CLASSICAL GUITAR
for the Steel-String Guitarist

William Tiger Fitzhugh

ISBN 978-1-4234-2847-3

HAL•LEONARD® CORPORATION

7777 W. BLUEMOUND RD. P.O. BOX 13819 MILWAUKEE, WI 53213

In Australia Contact:
Hal Leonard Australia Pty. Ltd.
4 Lentara Court
Cheltenham, Victoria, 3192 Australia
Email: ausadmin@halleonard.com.au

Visit Hal Leonard Online at
www.halleonard.com

CONTENTS

Page	Title	CD Tracks
4	**INTRODUCTION**	
	It's Just Different Strings, RIGHT?	
	The Plan	
7	**CHAPTER 1:** Playing Position	
8	**CHAPTER 2:** The Right Hand	
11	**CHAPTER 3:** Block Chords	1–8
19	**CHAPTER 4:** Thumb/Finger Alternation	9–16
27	**CHAPTER 5:** Simple Arpeggios	17–24
38	**CHAPTER 6:** Compound Arpeggios and Finger Alternation	25–31
48	**CHAPTER 7:** Alternation on a Single String	32
53	**CHAPTER 8:** Rest-Stroke ("Lead") Playing	33–35
58	**CHAPTER 9:** Slurs	36
59	**CHAPTER 10:** Trills	37–44
60	**AFTERWORD**	
61	**APPENDIX 1:** Positioning the Guitar	
62	**APPENDIX 2:** Major Scales	
64	**APPENDIX 3:** Repertoire for Gigs	

INTRODUCTION

Every classical-guitar method book that I have seen starts with the assumption that the reader has never picked up a guitar before. This book, however, is intended for guitarists who already play steel-string guitar and are interested in broadening their scope by playing classical guitar.

To me, the words "classical guitar" mean three things: 1) a *type* of guitar, 2) a *style* of music, and 3) a *technique* for guitar playing. The type of guitar is fairly objective: a wide and flat fingerboard, a neck that joins the body at the 12th fret, and nylon (or similar) strings. Some newer models have cutaways, and there are some hybrids with 14-fret necks and a narrower fingerboard. The style of music is primarily 19th-century classical music written by Fernando Sor, Mauro Giuliani, Dionisio Aguado, Fernando Carulli, Matteo Carcassi, Francisco Tarrega, and several other guitarist-composers, as well as works written for other instruments by such composers as Johann Sebastian Bach, Dominico Scarlatti, Fredric Chopin, and others. Although we will be playing (for the most part) classical music on a classical guitar, the technique that is addressed in this book is very similar to fingerstyle for steel-string guitar.

This is not a repertoire book; instead of teaching many different pieces of music, I use a small number of pieces in different contexts. Therefore, you can learn valuable pick-hand techniques without having to learn many different musical pieces. There are literally hundreds of repertoire books on the market, varying in difficulty and appeal. However, the main reason I am not including many pieces here is because you are learning a technique, not a style of music. The goal of music is to share it with others, and actually making a living at it is not too much to ask, either! When I am hired to play classical guitar, I invariably include some Beatles, some Gershwin, some jazz standards, and some folk/Celtic music. Hopefully, many of the songs you already know will lend themselves to this new style of playing. Believe me, the ability to play a gig completely solo is a huge advantage with respect to making a living as a guitarist.

It's Just Different Strings, RIGHT?

I learned how to play guitar, like most guitar players who learned in the sixties and early seventies, by experimentation, sharing information with friends, the occasional book, and using my ears (in my case, trying to play Beatles, Cream, and Neil Young). Later on, I attended Berklee College of Music for three invaluable years, studying guitar with John Damien and John Amaral, and learning things that, 30 years later, I am still trying to fully grasp. After an "extended summer vacation" of 17 years, I finished my B.S. in Classical Guitar Performance, studying with Dr. Stanley Yates, at Austin Peay State University in Clarksville, Tennessee, where I am currently finishing work on a master's degree. I am commencing this book with my own guitar history to show you that I came from a self-taught, steel-string background. Later, while still on steel-string, I continued my guitar instruction via a supervised, highly directed and organized approach before finally learning classical music and classical guitar.

My first bit of advice to those who are entering the world of classical guitar from a steel-string guitar perspective is *to throw away your metronome*! I do not mean this literally, of course, but all of the music that I had played previously, whether it was jazz, rock, country, blues, bluegrass, or any combination thereof, was primarily *dance* music—at least that was its tradition. (I realize, however, that probably very few people danced to King Crimson, Yes, or Jeff Beck). Of course, in order to play dance music well, the beat must be steady. Consequently, during my entire professional life, I strove to play with an "inner click track." Occasionally, there were *ritards* at the end of a song or at the end of a phrase, but these were rare. A great pop/jazz/rock musician can play for a very long time without varying the tempo at all.

When I first realized that I didn't want to be a 50-year-old rock 'n' roll guitar player (fine for an *artist*, but not so fine for a *sideman*), it wasn't hard to learn how to hold my right hand properly or to put the guitar on my left leg. What *was* difficult, however, was trying to understand what people meant when they told me to "hold this note for its full value" (was I supposed to cut the rest of them short?) or to "breathe a bit here" (should I hold my breath for the rest of the piece?). This is what I meant when I told you to "throw away your metronome": realize that the music has ebbs and flows, pulls and pushes, and that some notes really *do* mean more than others. I recall asking Dr. Yates in a moment of frustration, "Why don't you just tell me when to rush and when to drag!" Classical guitar is a whole different mind-set. It's neither better nor worse—it's just different.

One of the reasons I wanted to play classical guitar was that it is a self-contained, self-accompanied instrument. Solo jazz guitar, of course, is an established form and, in fact, shares much musical language with solo classical guitar. Many incredibly talented guitarists play unaccompanied on steel-string acoustic, such as Leo Kottke and the late Michael Hedges, but the idea of distinct lines, or voices, moving from one note to the next is fundamental to classical guitar. Many of the pieces you will be learning in this book do not have a distinct melody; rather, they are simply chord progressions. It is important to remember that these are, for the most part, *technical studies* that, while still beautiful pieces of music, are primarily written to help the student master the techniques needed to play more advanced pieces. Some pieces have separate bass lines and melody lines, often with harmony lines between them. *Counterpoint* is the term used to describe the event of separate lines moving against each other.

The second piece of advice I will offer is to remind the student that he/she is playing music written *by* someone else. When I play rock, country, or jazz music, I am almost always making up my own part to one degree or another. Even when I am playing musical theater, I am mostly playing from a page of chord symbols, and the specific voicings that I use are up to me. This is one advantage that commercial steel-string players have over players who are solely trained as classical players; many people who read *only* notes have no idea what a C9$\sharp$11 is, or even a simple C7, and thus are limited in their ability to create their own arrangements from lead sheets. When playing solo jazz guitar, chord-melody style, I am free to voice chords under the melody however I like, and this is what gives this style its freedom and ability to be expressive in so many ways. Classical guitar music, of course, also needs to be expressive, but we are expressing "musical" elements, like dynamics, phrasing, timbre, and voice-leading; the actual notes we are playing are written out, and everyone who plays the piece will be playing the exact same notes. It took me awhile to realize that, even if I was able to play a solo exactly like Eric Clapton did on *Disraeli Gears*, the chances were slim that even Eric Clapton would play that same solo note for note ever again. Most great rock music has at least some of the improvisational nature of jazz music, and a solo or an entire performance as recorded in a studio or live is only an audio photograph of that song *at that time*.

Playing a complete piece of music, without aid from other musicians, is a great feeling. While I felt very proud when I could play a Jimi Hendrix or a George Harrison solo note for note, I still knew that something was missing. A classical-guitar performance is a complete musical experience.

The Plan

This book is divided into short sections, each dealing with a specific aspect of classical guitar playing. Hopefully, you will be able to get through each section in one or two practice sessions.

CHAPTER 1
Playing Position

Playing classical guitar presents some unique challenges. It can be very "tricky" and detailed so we must do everything we can to make it as easy as possible. The goal of technique is always to make playing as easy as possible.

Correct positioning of the guitar makes it easier to play. When you stand up to play steel-string guitar (i.e., with a strap), notice that the soundhole and/or pickups are located in the center of the front of your body and the neck is pointed up slightly. This is the goal of proper positioning for the classical guitar as well. To achieve this, we sit on a chair and place the guitar on the left thigh; additionally, we elevate the left leg by placing the left foot on a footstool so that the neck of the guitar is angled upward. The soundhole should be positioned at the center of your torso, the highest part of the guitar body (the bass side) should be touching your chest, and the end of the guitar's body should be touching the inside of your right thigh.

Positioning of the Guitar

Sitting with footstool

Sitting with "neck-up" support

CHAPTER 2
The Right Hand

In classical-guitar terminology, the fingers of the right (pick) hand are each represented by a letter: *p* = thumb (from Spanish *pulgar*), *i* = index *(indicio)*, *m* = middle *(medio)*, *a* = ring *(anular)*. Although rarely used, the little (pinky) finger is represented by the letter *c* *(chico*, in homage to the Marx brothers). You probably already use your right-hand fingers to play guitar; many steel-string players use their middle and ring fingers, while holding the pick between their thumb and index fingers. Further, steel-string players will forgo a pick altogether—instead, using four (or even five) right-hand fingers. Generally, when one plays a steel-string guitar in either of these styles, the heel of the hand rests on the bridge or on the top of the guitar in such a way that only the middle joint of the fingers can move when plucking the strings. If a steel-string guitar is played with a thumb pick, the hand is generally held parallel to the top of the guitar.

Thumbpick

Flatpick

Fingerstyle

The strings of a classical guitar are further apart than those of a steel-string so the right-hand position needs to be altered to take advantage of this fact. A good way to correctly form the right-hand position is to hold a baseball or a rubber ball of equal size. Your hand should approximate this shape when you play classical guitar. Another way is to hold a ping-pong ball in your hand while you play the guitar (only until you get the feel of playing with your hand in the correct shape).

There are dozens of books with explanations of exactly how to form the correct hand position but, in reality, people have slight differences in their hand structure so it is *not* a case of "one size fits all." Here are some general guidelines and suggestions:

Too arched

Too flat

Correct

Make a light fist with your right (pick) hand. Relax your fingers so that they release slightly. Place *p* (thumb) on the fourth string, *i* (index) on the third string, *m* (middle) on the second string, and *a* (ring) on the first string. Push your arm out in front of you so that your wrist arches slightly and your knuckles are almost directly over your fingertips. Curl your fingertips back toward your elbow (make sure that they are flexed inward slightly, not straight; each segment of your finger should be flexed inward). Don't let your fingertips go "under" the strings more than a few millimeters; you don't wrap your fingers around the strings, you simply touch them very close to the fingertip.

When you look down on your right hand, you should see a slight "V" shape between your thumb and index fingers. If you do not see this, slide your fingers slightly towards the bridge of the guitar, keeping them on the strings. Your wrist should be arched so that it is slightly farther away from the guitar than your knuckles.

Next, make that light fist again, only this time pluck the strings as you do it. Make sure that the back of your hand remains straight and doesn't pull up (away) from the guitar; your hand should not change its angle relative to your forearm. Let your fingers push "through" the strings, touch the palm of your hand with your fingers, and let your thumb come to rest at about the middle joint of your index finger. In actual practice, the fingers will not touch the palm of the hand; this is to learn the motion. Once learned, simply let the fingers travel in as far as needed, without any effort to stop the motion. The side of your hand that is facing the guitar should appear almost flat. Congratulations! You just played an Em7 chord.

Now let your fingers and thumb release, and start the whole process over: place *i*, *m*, and *a* on the third, second and first strings, respectively, and place *p* on the fourth string. Make the light fist again, being sure that your wrist does not bend and force your fingers to point down (towards the treble strings). Your fingers should be about halfway between being parallel with the strings, and being at a right angle relative to them.

Example 1

In this sequence, we will *place* the fingers *a*, *m*, and *i* on their strings (high E, B, and G, respectively), *pluck* the fingers into the palm of the hand, *release* the fingers to near their starting position, and then *replace* the fingers on the strings. Rest your thumb on the D string.

Be sure that you don't *extend* (i.e., straighten out) your fingers when you release them; simply let them "fall out" from the palm of your hand, remaining slightly flexed (curled in).

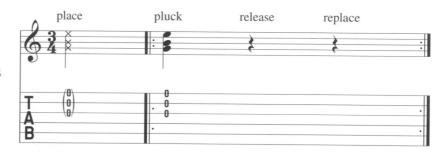

Right-hand preparation

Right hand after fingers pluck

Example 2

When plucking with the thumb *(p)*, think of it as simply touching your index finger between its tip joint and the middle joint. Do not try to stop the motion of the thumb; instead, simply start the motion and let the thumb come to rest on the index finger. Place your thumb on the D string.

Thumb after plucking

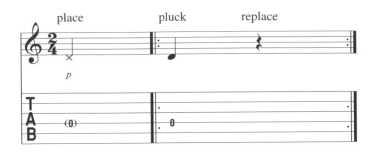

Your fingers should make contact with the strings at approximately the left (thumb) side of the fingers rather than the middle of the fingertips. Many players try to make contact with the strings where the flesh and the fingernail meet.

This brings up a whole new issue: the fingernails. There are many variations among the shapes of people's fingernails so no hard-and-fast rule applies. In general, there should be no sharp edges or steep angles on the left (thumb) side of your nail; these will "catch" on the string and impede the motion of pushing through the strings. File your nails so that the white part tapers to "nothing" on the left side of your fingers.

The aforementioned "light fist" movement is used for playing *block chords*; that is, chords with all of the notes sounded simultaneously. Following this section are several etudes for practicing this technique.

Standard practice with respect to written classical guitar music is to use circled numbers to indicate strings (① = high E, ② = B, ③ = G, ④ = D, ⑤ = A, ⑥ = low E) and un-circled numbers to indicate left-hand fingers (1 = index, 2 = middle, 3 = ring, 4 = little [pinky] finger). Consequently, classical-guitar notation can seem a little confusing at first. Another common practice is to have two stems attached to the same note. This occurs when a single note sounds as both the bass voice and as an "upper" voice. However, you simply play the note *once*. Here are two examples of different notation for the same music. The first example, with double stems, is much clearer and easier to read.

Dynamics is the term used to describe the loudness or softness of the music. $\boldsymbol{f}$ means loud (from *forte*, Italian for—you guessed it—loud) and $\boldsymbol{p}$ means soft (from *piano*, Italian for… go ahead, take a lucky guess). $\boldsymbol{m}$ means medium (*mezzo*), and is used before either $\boldsymbol{f}$ or $\boldsymbol{p}$ to mean "loud (or soft) but not *too* loud (or soft)." To indicate greater dynamic levels, we simply include the letter two or three times.

The dynamic range, then, from very, very soft to very, very loud is:

$$\boldsymbol{ppp} \quad \boldsymbol{pp} \quad \boldsymbol{p} \quad \boldsymbol{mp} \quad \boldsymbol{mf} \quad \boldsymbol{f} \quad \boldsymbol{ff} \quad \boldsymbol{fff}$$

CHAPTER 3
Block Chords

Block chords are simply chords in which all the notes are sounded at the same time. For example, strumming a chord quickly with a pick produces a block chord.

The following are two simple block-chord exercises. Pay close attention to the feel of your right hand; it should start as a "relaxed fist," with the appropriate fingers touching the appropriate strings, and then you should quickly close your fist so that your fingers push "through" the strings. Your thumb should come to rest at about the middle joint of your index finger, or just below (towards the fingertip). After sounding the chord, let your fingers and thumb relax and "fall away" from the palm of your hand. They should nearly come to rest over their corresponding strings; if they are too far to one side or the other, adjust your starting position so that when your fingers are relaxed, they naturally come to rest in proximity of the appropriate strings. Then, replace your fingers on the strings and restart start the process.

Example 3

> **NOTE:** In all examples, fingerings are indicated in the top (standard notation) staff.

You may have noticed that, when you place your fingers on the strings in preparation for the next pluck, the notes don't actually last as long as indicated (i.e., the strings are silenced when you place your fingers on them). While learning Chapter 3, you should *place* your fingers on the strings, and then *pluck* them. There will be a silence before you pluck; this is called *muting* the strings. This method is called a *prepared stroke* (you prepare your finger on the string before playing). In most musical contexts, you want to avoid muting.

The way to do this is by using a *continuity stroke*. Instead of touching the strings when you release your fingers, let them stop just *above* the string so that the only time they touch the strings is when they pluck them. This gives the music a full sound with one note leading directly to the next.

Play all of the block chords in Chapter 3 with the prepared stroke. After you finish, go back and play them again, this time using the continuity stroke exclusively.

In the following exercise, you will extend the right-hand thumb away from the hand in order to play the low E string. Don't let the tip of your thumb bend; instead, simply extend the whole thumb from the wrist joint.

Example 4

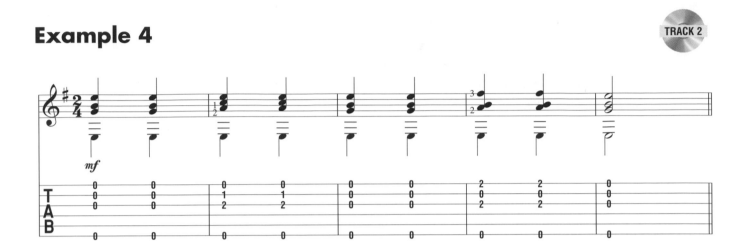

Example 5

Do not lift your left-hand fingers off their respective string if the next chord contains the same note, played with the same finger, as in Example 5. Here, the first finger remains on the C note on string 2 for the first four measures, and the fourth finger remains on the G note on string 1 in measures 5–7. This technique will help with speed and smoothness of chord-changing.

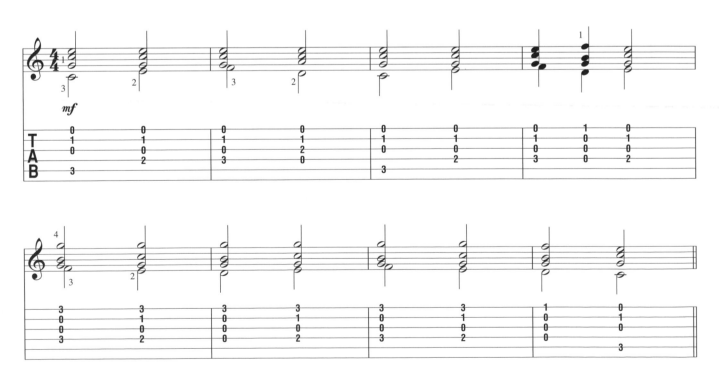

Example 6

Example 6 is based on an etude by Fernando Carulli and uses only the *p*, *i*, and *m* fingers. In this situation, bring the *a* finger slightly into the hand when you prepare the other fingers on the strings (as if you have just barely plucked the *a* finger) so that it is not touching the string, and then let it move into the palm of the hand with the other fingers.

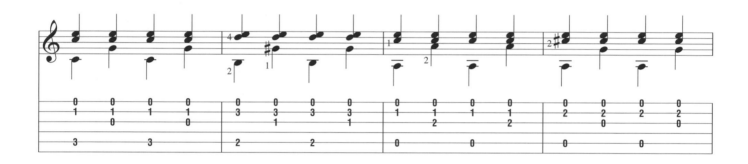

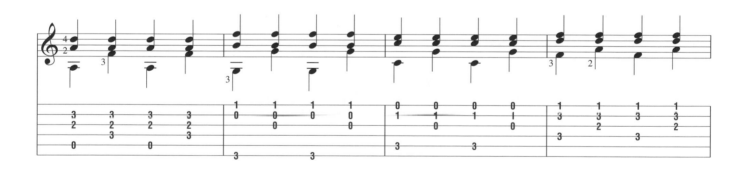

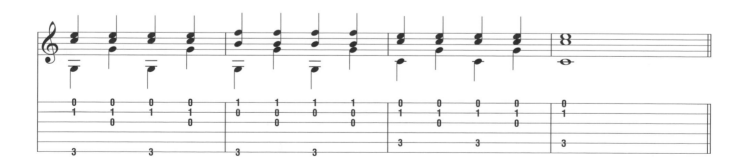

Example 7

Example 7 is based on an etude by Dionisio Aguado and, like Example 6, only uses the *p*, *i*, and *m* fingers. Notice that, despite the movement, the second finger of the left (fret) hand stays on string 3 for the duration of measures 1–4.

Example 8

Example 8, also based an etude by Carulli, uses all three right-hand fingers along with the thumb. Remember, move all of your fingers at once, and when you finish the stroke, your hand should be in a light fist. Your left hand will make a *barre chord* in this piece; these are indicated by the letter "C," followed by a Roman numeral that indicates which fret to bar. If the bar is less than a full bar (all six strings), it is usually indicated by "1/2 C," which usually means anywhere from two to five strings are covered by the first finger. However, many editors now favor a more exact method, namely 4/6 for the top four strings, 3/6 for the top three strings, and so on. Others use just a single number. For example, "C III²" indicates that the highest two strings are barred at the third fret.

Playing full barre chords on a classical guitar can be a challenge. Keep the index finger of your left hand *absolutely straight* so that you could put a straight edge from your knuckle to your fingernail; you may want to bend your wrist a bit more than usual, however. You may also want to roll your finger out a bit, in the direction of the thumb, so that you are fretting the strings slightly on the side of your finger, rather than the bottom. Be sure not to flex the tip of your finger; this will only push the rest of your finger away from the strings.

Example 9

Example 9 is based on Mauro Giuliani's Opus 48, #5. This piece introduces us to *shifting position*; that is, moving the left hand smoothly up and down the neck. Before you shift, you should always have a clear understanding of where you are going *before* you begin the shift. Look at the fret to which you will be moving, not at your hand's current position. Release pressure with your fingers and thumb, maintaining very light contact with the strings. After you are able to do this easily, you may want to release contact entirely on the bass strings to avoid the scratchy sound of your fingers rubbing the winding of the string. With your shoulder, move your upper arm in, toward your body, to move up the neck, and out, away from your body, to move down the neck. Your left hand should remain in a *parallel position* in this piece; that is, the palm of the hand is roughly parallel with the neck. Therefore, your fingers will be roughly parallel with the frets.

To see the difference between *parallel position* and *rotated position*, play a first-position G major chord with fingers 3, 2, and 4, low to high. This puts your hand in parallel position. Now, play either a D major chord with fingers 1, 3, and 2, low to high, or another G major, but this time with fingers 2, 1, and 3, low to high. This puts your hand in a rotated position. Be sure that your thumb is centered on the back of the neck and not sticking over the edge toward the low E string.

In some of the chords in Example 9, individual notes are played on more than one string; thus, some chords have only three notes, even though four strings are being plucked. These notes are notated with two noteheads. Pay attention to the third finger of the left (fret) hand; it remains on the D string throughout measures 1–8.

Example 10 - *A Minor Consideration*

TRACK 8

Example 10 is a simple musical piece that uses block chords exclusively. Notice the dynamics in this song; the < and > symbols between the staves are *crescendi* and *decrescendi*, respectively. A crescendo indicates an increase in volume, and a decrescendo indicates a decrease in volume. Volume is mostly affected by the speed with which you pluck the strings; a very quick motion produces a louder sound. You'll notice on the CD I play some of the chords with a "rolling" style. More on this technique later.

The double bar lines at the end of measures 4 and 12 indicate that one section of music ends and another is about to begin. Also, notice the mark over the half note at the end of measure 4. This is a *fermata*, which indicates that the note is to be held "out of time" (i.e., without counting). Think of "The Star-Spangled Banner": "O'er the land of the *freeeeeeeee...*"

Now go back to the beginning of Chapter 3 and play the all of the Examples again, this time using the continuity stroke. Unless otherwise stated, the continuity stroke will be the technique used for the rest of the book. Unless you need to silence a string before you play it again (for example, if the chord changes and the previous open string clashes with the new chord), the continuity stroke is almost always used. Of course, if you are fingering the string with your left hand, you can simply release pressure on the string to silence the note. Be sure to do that quickly, just like on a steel-string guitar; if you release the string slowly, you will hear a buzz.

CHAPTER 4
Thumb/Finger Alternation

Thumb/finger alternation is basically the bass/strum ("boom-chick") pattern that is used on steel-string guitar. Instead of playing the bass note with the pick, and then strumming the rest of the chord, we play the bass note with our thumb and pluck the remaining two or three fingers together, as one unit.

Too straight

Too flexed

Correct

Hold your left (fret) hand in front of you, palm facing the floor. Imagine that you have an insect bite on the back of that hand, and scratch the imaginary bite with the *i* and *m* fingers of your right (pick) hand. Your natural tendency is probably to hold your fingers slightly curved, yet not very tight. (Note: You should be moving your fingers from the knuckle of the middle joint.) Experiment with your right-hand placement, moving it closer to and then farther away from your left hand. Notice how your fingers either straighten (extend) or collapse (flex). The ideal position for playing guitar is about halfway between completely straight and completely flexed. Each joint in your fingers (knuckle, middle, and tip joints) should be about halfway between the two extremes.

Now pick up your guitar (while remembering what was said concerning placement of the guitar) and rest your right thumb on the A string. Prepare your right hand exactly as we did for the block chords: *i* on string 3, *m* on string 2, and *a* on string 1. Leaving your thumb on the A string, mimic the scratching motion with the remaining fingers. You should have just heard the Em chord again; this time, without the minor 7th, since your thumb didn't pluck the D string. Your fingers should end up inside the palm of your hand. As you did before, release your fingers and let them "fall out" of the palm of your hand, stopping (without effort) just above their respective strings. If your fingers do not end up just over the strings, adjust your starting hand position.

The right-hand fingers are not always used simultaneously; many times, *i–m*, *i–a*, or *m–a* are used. This is achieved by curling the unused finger into the hand slightly, as if it has just plucked the string. Play the following examples with the appropriate fingers; be sure to keep *p* on the A string.

Example 11

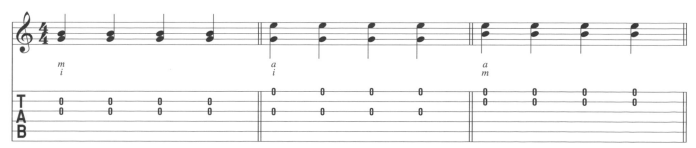

Example 12

To pluck solely with your thumb, rest the *i*, *m*, and *a* fingers on the G, B, and high E strings, respectively, and *p* on the D or A strings. Form your hand with correct technique, as previously described. Now push your thumb through the string and let it come to rest at the middle joint—or just below the middle joint—of the *i* finger. Your thumb should end up slightly farther away from the guitar than before the stroke. Don't try to stop the motion of your thumb; instead, let it move at full speed until it makes contact with your *i* finger. (This same idea is true of the other fingers when they are playing at the same time. Think of it as turning on a light switch—it is either "on" or "off"; the movement between the two is immediate.)

Example 13

First, let's play Example 13 to simply get used to alternating between the thumb and the fingers, and then we will play the examples from previous chapters, but instead of block chords, we will use this right-hand pattern. Using the prepared stroke, slowly repeat this exercise, following this pattern:

1) *p* plucks (comes to rest on *i*)
2) *i*, *m*, and *a* pluck; at the same time, *p* releases and touches the D string
3) *p* plucks and comes to rest against the *i* finger at the same time that *i*, *m*, and *a* release and touch the G, B, and high E strings, respectively

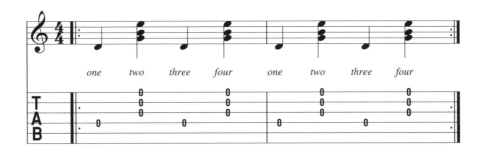

> **NOTE:** For the rest of the book, I will refer to strings by their number:
> high E = string 1, B = string 2, G = string 3, D = string 4, A = string 5, and low E = string 6

We will now play the etudes from previous chapters by using the alternating *p–ima* pattern. There is something new for the left hand, though: *sequential placement*. This means that instead of placing your left-hand fingers down on all of the notes simultaneously, as we would if we were strumming a steel-string or playing block chords, we will place our left-hand fingers on the strings at the exact time that we pluck those strings with our right-hand fingers. This is a very important technique! Our left-hand fingers almost always go from one note to another note when we change chords. Thus, it is impossible to replace all of your fingers smoothly. This technique, however, allows us to play the note with both hands. It will improve your time-keeping and help you to play more *legato* (i.e., smoothly). It is the same principle as clapping your hands. You don't think: "I must move my left hand towards my right hand and somehow, at the same time, move my right hand towards my left hand." It is simply a single action that involves *both* hands. As you play the following group of exercises, be sure that your left-hand fingers are placed on the notes at the exact same time that note is plucked; of course, this means that if more than one fretted note is being played by the *i–m–a* combination, those left-hand fingers will be placed together.

The notation of this type of rhythm can look confusing. It is usually written "one-and, two-and," with the "and" note (the note played on the offbeat) occasionally cut shorter than notated in order to make a smooth chord transition. Remember, music is ultimately about *hearing* rather than *seeing*; thus, play it gracefully and musically.

In Examples 14–16, the thumb plays beats 1 and 3; the fingers play beats 2 and 4.

Example 14

TRACK 9

Example 15

TRACK 10

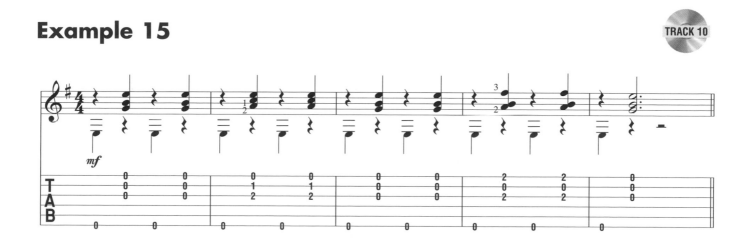

Example 16

Example 17

In Example 17, the beat is divided in half. Count: "one-and, two-and, three-and, four-and". The thumb plays beats 1, 2, 3, and 4, and the fingers play all of the "ands." The ties that are attached to the last note of each measure indicate that the notes continue to sound until the next time you touch the strings with your fingers.

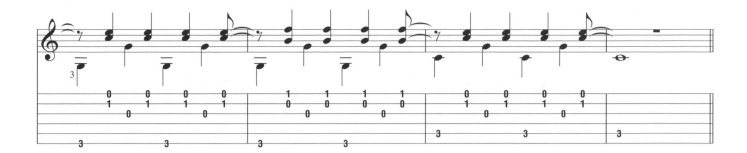

Example 18

Example 18 is notated more "correctly" than Examples 17 and 19. The notes at the end of the measure are tied to the first notes of the next measure (they are not re-plucked). Play these chords the same way as you did in Example 17: pluck the strings on the "and" of beat 2, and let them ring until the "and" of beat 1 of the next measure. Count: "one-and, two-and, one-and, two-and," etc.

Example 19

Example 20

Example 20 is written in 4/4 time, meaning that there are four quarter notes in each measure. Examples 18 and 19 were written in 2/4 time, meaning there are two quarter notes in each measure. Notice that the notes that the fingers play on the "and" of beat 2 are tied to those same notes on beat 3. Do not pluck these notes again (on beat 3); this is the same idea as tying notes across the bar line. Music in 4/4 time is often written this way to make it easier to see the middle of the measure. Although it may look confusing at first, this notation style actually makes the music much easier to read. Play Example 20 the same way as you played Example 17: the thumb playing beats 1, 2, 3, and 4, and the fingers playing all of the "ands."

Example 21 - *November*

Play Example 21 with *p–ima* alternation, paying strict attention to the indicated dynamics.

CHAPTER 5
Simple Arpeggios

Arpeggios are chords sounded one note at a time. With a pick, we simply strum the strings slowly to achieve this; in classical playing, we use one finger at a time. Simple arpeggios are chords played in sequence, from low note to high or from high note to low. Compound arpeggios are chords played in any other sequence.

Classical-guitar music is full of arpeggios. In fact, arpeggios are probably the most important musical texture for classical guitar. Arpeggios allow guitarists to combine harmony with rhythm (e.g., "Stairway to Heaven" begins with an A minor arpeggio). The technique for the left hand is pretty much the same as it was for the *p–ima* alternation: place your left-hand fingers on the notes at the exact time that you pluck those notes with your right-hand fingers. For arpeggios, it is the right hand that must play a new pattern.

There are two types of arpeggios: *simple* and *compound*. You will learn simple arpeggios in this section. A simple arpeggio is any pattern in which the *i*, *m*, and *a* fingers pluck, in order, from *i* to *a* or from *a* to *i*, whether all three fingers are used or not, and *p* plucks at the beginning or at the end of this sequence. This includes *p–i–m–a*, *a–m–i–p*, *p–a–m–i*, *a–m–i–p*; *p–i–m*, *m–i–p*, *p–m–i*, *i–m–p*; *p–i–a*, *a–i–p*, *p–a–i*, *i–a–p*; *p–m–a*, *a–m–p*, *p–a–m*, and *m–a–p*. Compound arpeggios are any arpeggios that "jump" between fingers, whether they change the order of the fingers (for example, *p–i–a–m*) or repeat the pattern "backwards" (*p–i–m–a–m–i*).

As your fingers come into the palm of your hand, they should remain there until the last finger is played. As the last finger is plucked, the thumb returns to its respective string; when the thumb is played, the fingers, as a group, return to their respective strings.

Play all of the examples in this chapter with the prepared stroke (i.e., after the last finger plucks, prepare the thumb; after the thumb plucks, prepare all the fingers together, as a group). After you finish, go back and play them all with the continuity stroke.

While voicing the C chord from above, play the following finger patterns with *p* on string 5, *i* on string 3, *m* on string 2, and *a* on string 1. Be sure that, as the last finger plucks, the thumb returns, and as the thumb plucks, the fingers return. Keep all of your fingers inside your hand until you release them all simultaneously.

p–i–m–a, a–m–i–p, p–a–m–i, i–m–a–p

p–i–m, m–i–p, p–m–i, i–m–p

p–i–a, a–i–p, p–a–i, i–a–p

p–m–a, a–m–p, p–a–m, m–a–p

Example 22

In Example 22 (as in all of the simple arpeggio examples), be sure to *release* and *replace* your right-hand fingers as one group when your thumb plucks; it is not necessary to dampen the bass strings with your thumb. Also, be sure to place your left-hand fingers at exactly the same time as you pluck the string with your right hand. Consequently, you may need to prepare your left-hand finger by lifting it from the previous note a bit early. The timing of the lifting and placing of the left-hand fingers is indicated in Example 22 only; use the same method for all of the arpeggio studies.

Example 23

In Example 23, the second finger of the left hand stays on the fourth-string E note throughout the whole song.

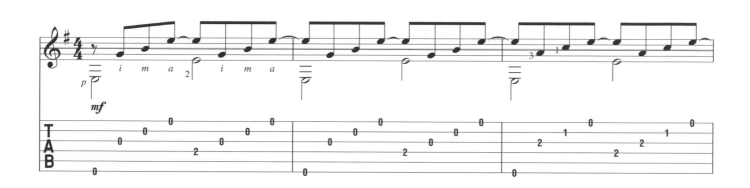

Example 24

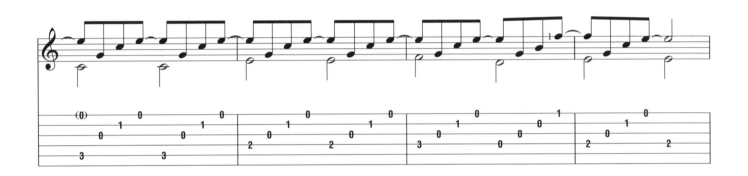

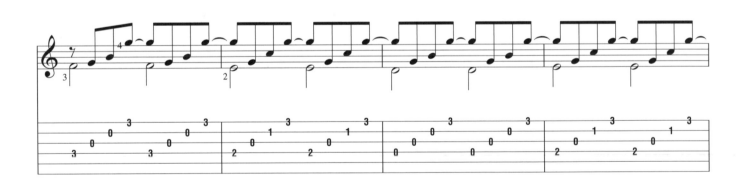

Example 25 - *Prelude Op. 114*

Example 25 ends with a five-note chord. In this case, it is played by the thumb (*p*) sweeping across the strings, as indicated by the curvy line next to the chord. The chord could also be sounded by the thumb playing strings 5 and 4, and the fingers playing strings 1–3.

By Fernando Carulli

*Simile (*sim.*) means to continue in the same manner; in this case, continue playing triplets.

When a left-hand finger plays a new note on the same string as the previous note, do not lift and replace the finger; instead, simply release pressure on the string and move the finger up or down the string to the new note, keeping minimal contact with the string.

Example 26

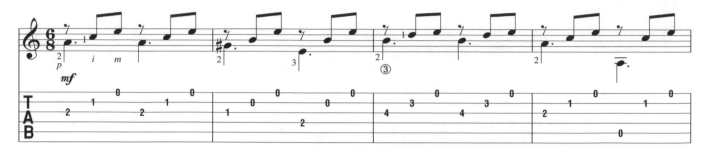

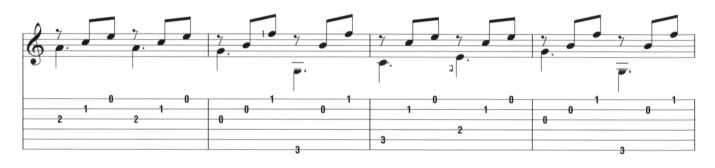

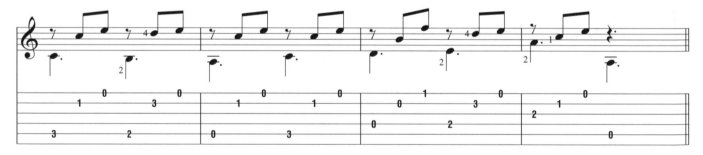

Example 27

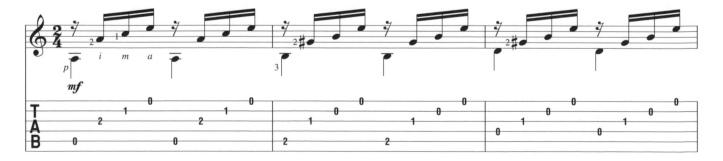

Example 28

TRACK 23

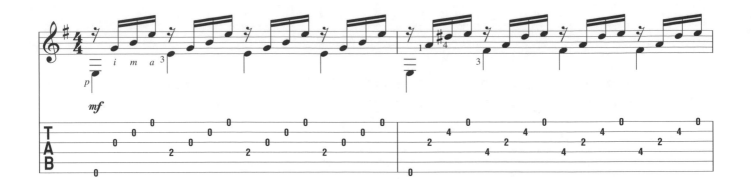

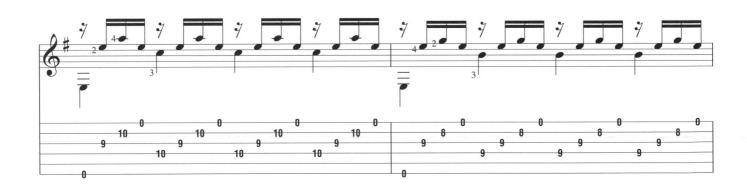

Example 29 - *Jarun*

Example 29 has a few things worth mentioning. The time signature is 6/8, meaning there are six eighth notes in each measure. Instead of counting "one, two, three, four, five, six," 6/8 is counted in "two"; "*one*, two, three, *four*, five, six." Two "big" beats are divided into three parts. In measures 9–11, move your left forearm from a parallel position to a rotated position and then back, holding fingers 1 and 3 in place and letting fingers 2 and 4 slide along the strings.

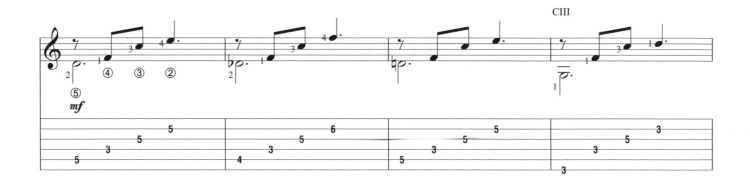

Now go back to the beginning of this chapter and play the examples with the continuity stroke.

CHAPTER 6
Compound Arpeggios and Finger Alternation

In order to play compound arpeggios correctly and easily, you must first learn how to alternate your right-hand fingers. This simply means that as one finger plucks, the other releases from inside the hand. Play Example 30 and pay close attention to your right hand, making sure you use one motion of the pluck and the release. Again, think about clapping your hands: Instead of two discrete actions, you're "alternating"—*in* with one finger, *out* with the other.

Example 30

Example 30 starts with *i* on the third string and *m* on the second. Pluck *i* in, and keep it inside your hand; then, pluck *m* in, and, at the same time you pluck *m*, release *i*, keeping *m* inside your hand. Next, pluck *i* and release *m*. Remember, this exchange of fingers should feel like *one motion*—just like walking.

Notice that the *a* finger moves in with the *m* finger. This is normal. Also, when one of these fingers is released from inside the hand, the other one will naturally release with it. The *i* finger has more independence than *a* or *m*.

Examples 31 & 32

Next, we will do the same action, but using different finger combinations: *i* and *a*, and *m* and *a*.

Be sure to repeat each of the previous examples until they feel completely natural and like one motion. All compound arpeggios are combinations of these motions. For example, a very common one is *p–i–m–a–m–i*, which follows this pattern:

1) *p*, *i*, *m*, and *a* each on their respective string (depending on what notes are being played)
2) *p* plucks
3) *i* plucks and remains in
4) *m* plucks and remains in
5) *a* plucks and remains in; *m* and *i* release
6) *m* plucks and remains in
7) *i* plucks and remains in; *p* releases
8) *p* plucks and remains in; *i*, *m*, and *a* release

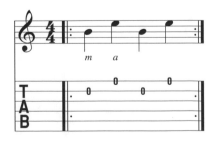

NOTE: *In these compound-arpeggio patterns, it is not necessary to hold "p" in until just before it plucks again; it can be released any time during the pattern.*

Example 33

Example 34

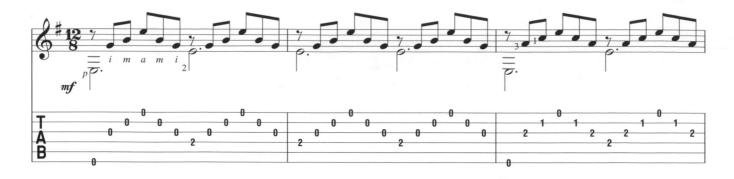

Example 35

Example 35 uses a slightly different pattern:

1) *p*, *i*, *m*, and *a* each on their respective string (in this case, fifth or fourth string, third string, second string, and first string, respectively)
2) *p* plucks
3) *i* plucks and remains in
4) *m* plucks and remains in; *i* releases (*a* moves in with *m*)
5) *i* plucks and remains in; *m* and *a* release
6) *a* plucks and remains in; *i* releases (*m* moves in with *a*)
7) *i* plucks and remains in; *m* and *a* release
8) *m* plucks and remains in; *i* releases
9) *i* plucks and remains in; *m* and *a* release
10) *p* plucks and remains in; *i* releases

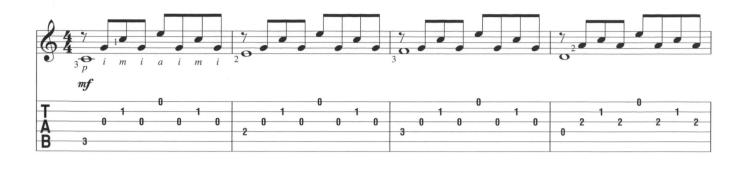

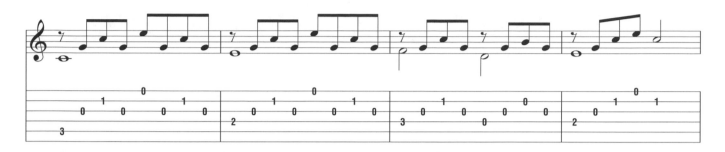

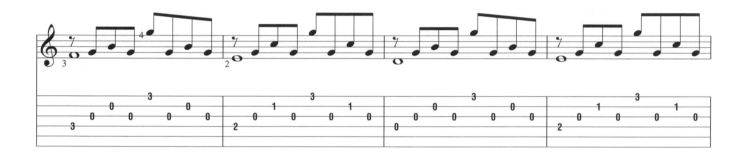

Example 36 - *Study in A Minor*

Example 36 is actually a bit simpler than the preceding ones. This pattern is:

1) *p*, *i*, and *m* each on their respective string (in this case, fifth, fourth, or third string; second string; and first string; respectively)
2) *p* plucks
3) *i* plucks and remains in
4) *m* plucks and remains in; *i* releases
5) *i* plucks and remains in
6) *p* plucks; *i* and *m* release

By Dionisio Aguado

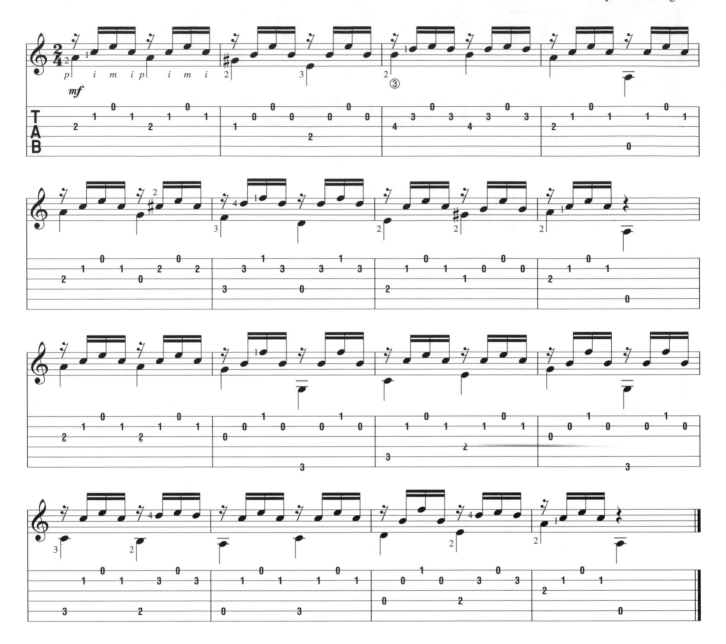

Example 37 - *Prelude in A Minor, Opus 114 #7*

TRACK 29

In the next prelude, Example 37, notice the left-hand fingering going from measure 1 to measure 2. If you tried to play it intuitively, voicing the E chord with your first and second fingers, the last note of the A minor chord (third-string A, measure 1) would be cut short because the finger playing that note must be lifted and moved to the B note on the fifth string. This situation happens often, so some chord fingerings will seem unusual. In this case, the second finger remains on the third string for the first eight measures.

By Fernando Carulli

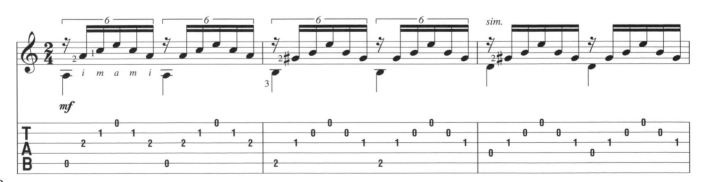

Example 38 - Allegro Opus 48, #5

Example 38 uses a technique called *campanella*, which involves fingering a note on a lower string to sound higher than the string above it (e.g., fingering an F on string 2 and playing string 1 [E] open). *Campanella* means "bell-like," and it sounds like an old bell tower, with all the notes cascading into each other. It is a beautiful sound (as you will hear) and is used often in classical guitar. When you do not want any note clashes, do not use this technique. But if you are after an open-ringing texture (much like using the sustain pedal on a piano), it is a great trick to know. You may even want to re-finger some songs that you already know to achieve this sound. The *campanella* technique can be very confusing, however. According to your right-hand's pattern, what should be a low-to-high run of notes is instead the exact opposite. Nonetheless, be sure to stay strictly with the right-hand fingering.

By Mauro Giuliani

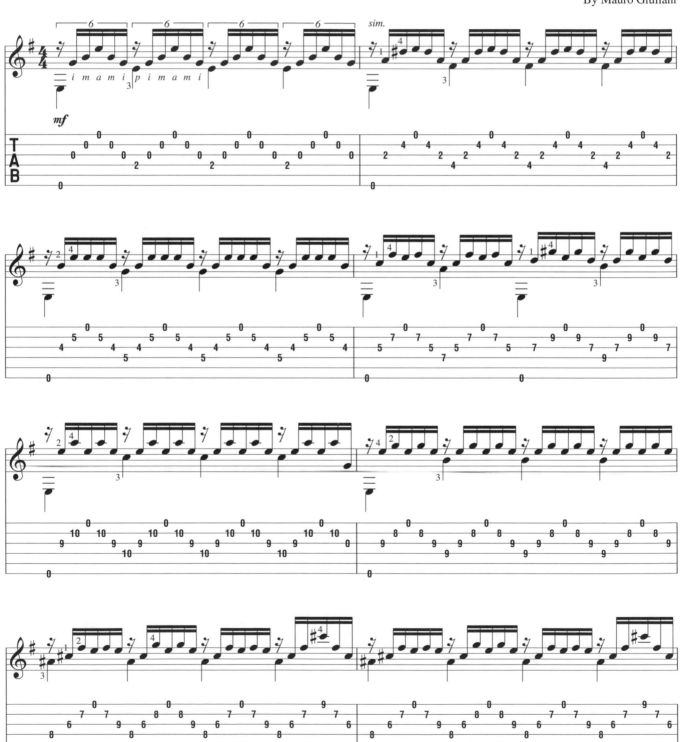

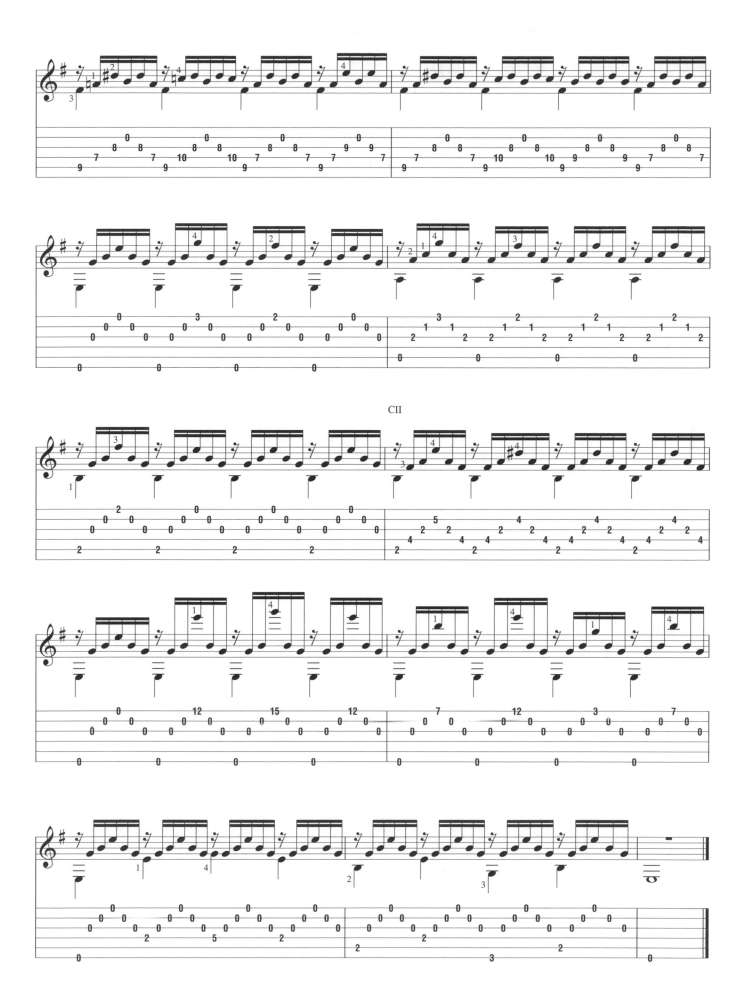

CII

Example 39 - *Winter Light*

Example 39 also uses campanella extensively, as well as dynamic contrast in repeated sections. From measure 1 to measure 2, *i*, *m*, and *a* move from strings 1, 2, and 3 to strings 2, 3, and 4 while the thumb remains on string 5. Measures 19–20 require you to move your elbow sharply in towards (and probably touching) your stomach. Keep your fourth finger arched and firmly on the F note (string 2), letting your first finger slide from Bb (string 3, measure 18) to A (string 3, measure 19). The last chord is written with grace notes (notes that sound immediately before the beat), which is an alternate way of writing the effect of "rolling" the chord. Notice the *ritard* in measure 39. This alerts the reader to gradually slow down till the end of the piece.

CHAPTER 7
Alternation on a Single String

The motion that is used to play more than one note on a single string is basically the same motion that is used to play arpeggios, only the right-hand fingers play on the same string. A good way to learn this movement is to hold your right hand in position as if you were playing guitar, but without the guitar (i.e., "air classical guitar"). The palm side of your hand and the underside of your forearm should be facing your torso. Now "drop" your hand by rotating your forearm in and bending your wrist slightly, keeping your arm at the same height as it was earlier. Your fingers should still be curved in, forming a light fist. Now the palm of your hand and the underside of your forearm should be facing approximately toward your belt, not completely facing the floor, but about half way between your torso and the floor. Rotate your arm back to your starting (arpeggio) position, and then let your hand "drop" a few more times to get the feel of it.

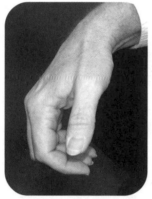

Chord/arpeggio position

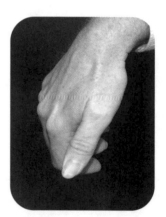

Single-string alternation position

Next, pick up your guitar and place it in the correct position. Place your right hand in the arpeggio position: keeping your thumb on the A or D string, lift your fingers *slightly* off the strings, letting your hand "drop," as before. If necessary, curl your fingers slightly in so that all three of your fingers (*i*, *m*, and *a*) are touching the third string.

Chord/arpeggio position

Single-string alternation position

Pluck these fingers in that order (you should hear the G note played three times quickly and in succession). Also, reverse the pattern and play *a*, *m*, and *i*. Now alternate the *i* and *m* fingers: just as we did playing arpeggios, as one finger plucks in, the other releases, creating a "walking" motion. Do this with *m* and *a* as well. This method is used in much the same way as alternating down/up strokes with a pick.

Example 40

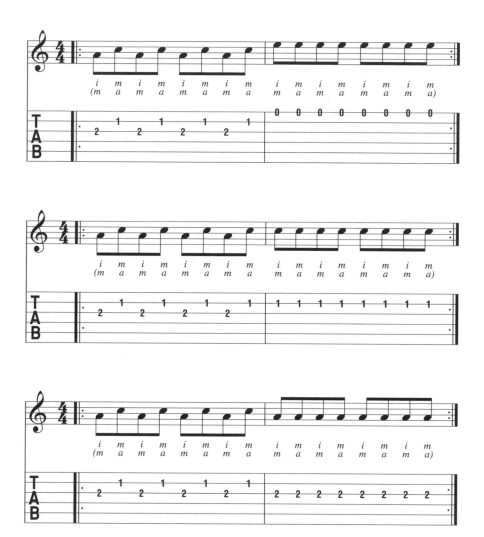

Example 41

Rest your thumb on string 5 and repeat these examples. Play them with *m* and *a* as well.

String Crossing

When moving from one string to the next, let the entire forearm pivot from the elbow so that the hand remains in a consistent position. Do not extend the fingers when moving to a higher string, or pull the fingers into the palm of the hand when moving to a lower string.

Example 42

Play Example 42 moving your arm from the elbow each time an asterisk (*) appears.

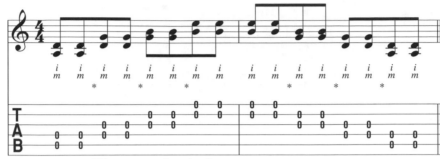

*Move your arm from the elbow.

Examples 43A–B illustrate different ways of crossing from one string to the next by using the two different hand positions. Example 43A is played with the hand in the single-string position and with the arm moving down after each finger has played the string. Example 43B is a much easier way to cross from string to string; the *m* finger is already above the higher string when the *i* finger plucks (when ascending), and the *i* finger is already over the lower string when the *m* finger plucks (when descending). Whenever possible, try to work out your right-hand fingering so that this "leading finger" method can be used; it is not always possible, but it makes it much easier. The *a* finger is often used to cross to the higher string when the *m* finger has just played. Try to play the lower string with the *m* finger and the higher string with the *i* finger to see just how much easier the leading-finger method makes it.

Example 43A

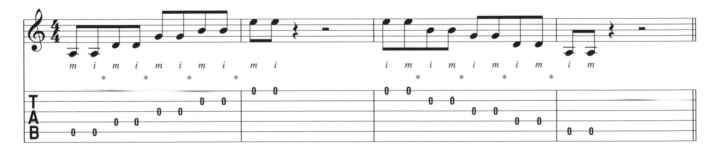

Example 43B

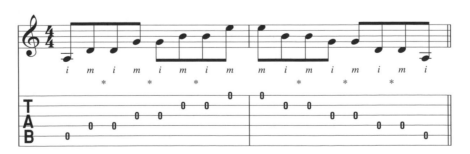

50

Example 44 - *Circus*

Example 44 is an easy waltz with short scale passages that are followed by block chords. To play the scale passages, let your wrist "drop" using the method that was mentioned earlier, and return your wrist to the starting position to play the chords. Notice that there are two dynamic indications; to bring out the melody, play the melody notes loudly and the harmony more softly. Melodic lines are generally written with the stems up.

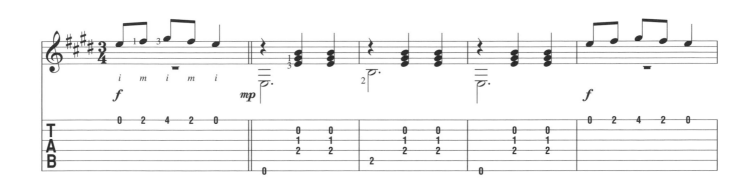

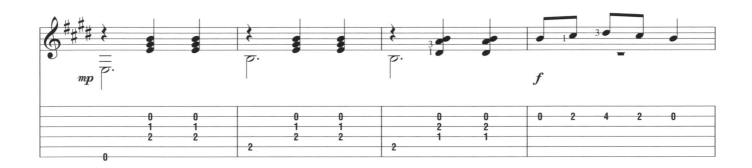

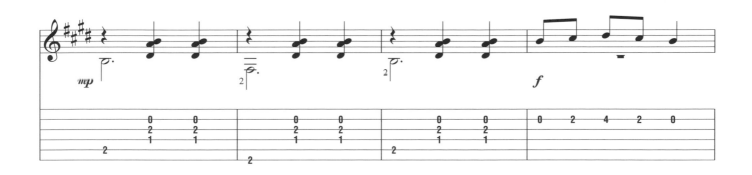

CHAPTER 8
Rest-Stroke ("Lead") Playing

While playing Example 44, you may have noticed that even though different dynamic levels (volumes) are indicated for the melody part and the chords, it was hard to play those dynamics because there is not a lot of difference between the two. All of the musical pieces that have been presented up to this point were basically "rhythm guitar" (well, rhythm and bass in Chapter 4). When melodies are played along with chords, it is like playing lead and rhythm guitar simultaneously. This is one of the great things about classical guitar—it's a one-man band!

The technique for playing "lead" on classical guitar is almost always a *rest stroke*. This technique is called a "rest stroke" because the finger comes to a rest on the next lower string. Rest strokes produce a louder and thicker sound than the chord/arpeggio stroke (called a *free stroke*) that we have been using till now. (You could think of rest strokes as sounding like humbuckers, and free strokes like single-coil pickups). Rest strokes are often used for playing scale passages and for "bringing out" (i.e., making louder) a particular note or group of notes.

Lay your hand on any flat surface (a tabletop or the back of your guitar would be good). While keeping the heel of your hand and your fingertips in contact with the surface, curl your fingers in to form a cupped hand. Now tap your *i* finger on the surface. Notice that the motion is mostly from your knuckle joint. This is the motion that is used to play a rest stroke.

To position the right hand to play rest strokes, place the *i* finger on the third string, as if you were preparing to play a free stroke, and, without changing any other aspect of the hand, extend the *i* finger to the first string. Using the motion that was used for tapping your finger, push your *i* finger down towards the body of the guitar, as if you were trying to touch the top (soundboard) of the guitar. The finger should come to a stop by touching the second string slightly farther away from the very tip of your finger than where the first string touched the finger. Place your *m* finger on the first string and play it the same way. Both of your fingers should now be resting on the second string. Now raise your *i* finger and place it on the first string again. As you press down, raise your *m* finger so that only one finger is touching the second string at any one time, and continue this pattern, alternating fingers. You may find this easier if you tilt the thumb side of your hand towards the top of the guitar slightly, and if you straighten your *i* finger slightly more than your *m* finger. While playing single-note melodies, rest your thumb on one of the bass strings. (Rest strokes are also the best way to play bass guitar.)

Hand Positions for Rest Stroke

Before rest stroke   *After rest stroke*

To play a rest stroke on the bass strings, generally you will use your thumb and push through the string, coming to rest on the next higher string. You may find that tilting the little-finger side of your hand towards the top of the guitar will help to correctly position your thumb.

Thumb rest stroke

Example 45

Play Example 45 by using rest strokes.

*Simile (*sim.*) means to continue in the same manner; in this case, continue alternating *i* and *m*.

Now go back and play Examples 41 and 44 using rest strokes for the melody (the single-note lines) and free strokes for the chords. You will notice that, without even trying, the melody sounds different than the chords. It is not necessary to play the rest strokes more forcefully than the free strokes; they will sound fuller and more distinct regardless. In fact, rest strokes can actually be played very softly; you have much more control over the volume with rest strokes. Of course, you can play the melody louder than the chords.

Rest strokes are almost always used to play scale passages. To improve this technique, play all of the scales in Appendix 2. Practice using either the fingers or the thumb on the bass strings; both techniques are used, depending on the context. Just keep in mind that a rest stroke with the fingers will mute the next lower string as the finger rests against it, and a rest stroke with the thumb will mute the next higher string. Check out Example 46 for a good representation of the scale passage idea in a musical context.

Example 46 - *Variations on "La Folia"*

TRACK 33

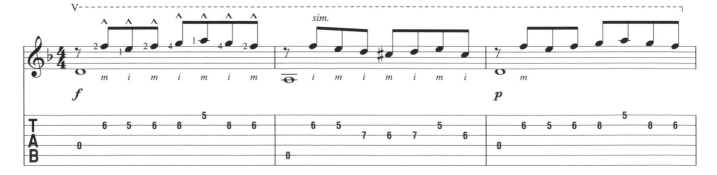

Example 47

Simultaneously playing a rest stroke with a finger and a free stroke with the thumb takes a bit of practice, but it is a very important tool. Keep the hand in its rest-stroke position and, as you pluck the thumb, bring it "up" a bit more than usual, away from the guitar. Your thumb should touch (or almost touch) your *i* finger closer to the knuckle than it would if you were playing all free strokes. There are different ways to indicate a rest stroke. Personally, I feel that it is a musical decision best left to the player, but when a rest stroke is written it is often indicated by a *marcato*, or "carrot" mark.

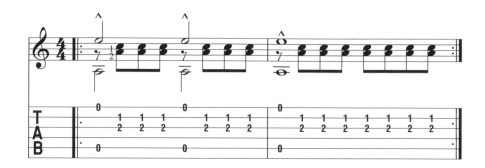

Because *a* is playing a rest stroke while *p* is playing a free stroke, *a* may sound a bit later than *p* if it gets "caught" on the string. To avoid this, stiffen *a* slightly more than usual. Of course, this may be the effect you want; delaying the melody a tiny bit helps to bring attention to it. But, as always, let the end result be for a *musical* reason, not a technical one.

Example 48 - *Conversation*

In Example 48, remember what we said about "playing the notes with both hands." Don't place the left-hand fingers that are playing the harmony until you are ready to play them with your right hand (on the "and" of beat 1). In the next-to-last measure, you will need to place your first finger right on the beat, as it plays at the same time as the melody. Be sure to make that shift smoothly, and to not place fingers 2 and 3 on the strings until the "and" of beat 3. Even though measures 4 and 8 are identical chords, I have fingered them differently to make the full bar in measure 9 easier to get to. Also, notice that in measure 9 *a* moves from string 1 to string 2, and *m* and *i* move from strings 2–3 to strings 3–4.

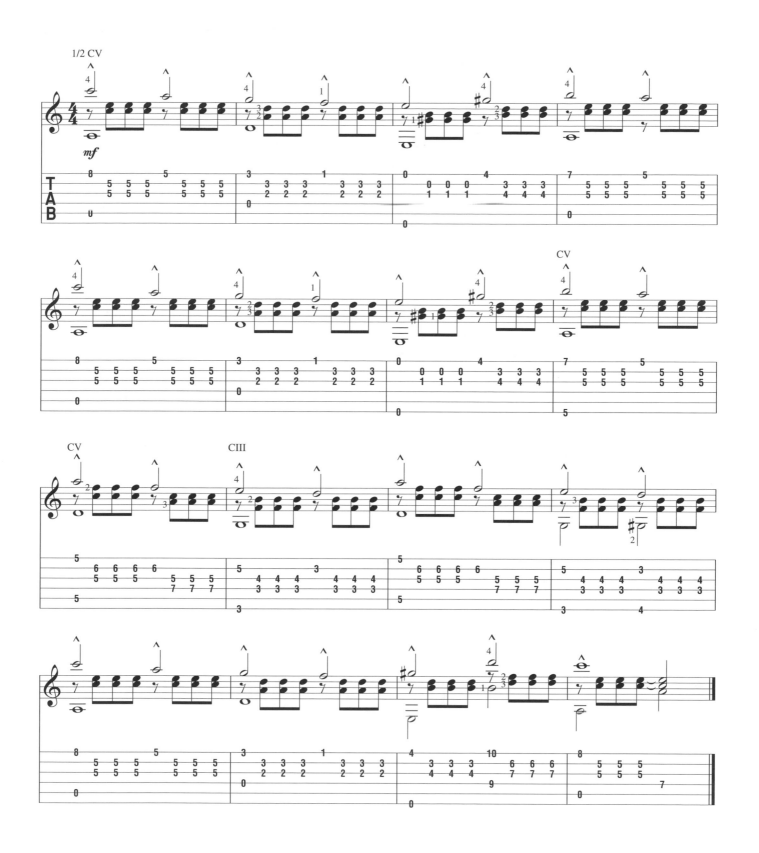

One final yet very important word about rest strokes: Now that you know what they sound like, try to match that sound with a free stroke. While there are many cases in which nothing but a rest stroke will suffice, you may find that simply playing louder (i.e., quicker and stiffer) and with more flesh (less nail) with your melody finger will present the same effect as a rest stroke, and can be used in more situations. Try it—go back and play Examples 47 and 48 this way.

CHAPTER 9
Slurs

A "slur" is another word for "hammer-on" and/or "pull-off." A hammer-on is an *ascending slur*, and a pull-off is a *descending slur*. Slurs are played the same way on a classical guitar as they are on a steel-string guitar. In both cases, be sure to hammer on from directly above the string (so that your finger moves in a straight line down to the neck) and pull off by flexing your finger, pulling it away from the string and towards the palm of your left hand. When you articulate a note *only* by hammering on, without plucking the string with your right hand, it is often indicated by "Played with left hand only." or "l.h.". In notation, slurs either connect the noteheads or are placed above the notes, on the stems.

Many people, myself included, have a bad habit of rushing the slur; that is, playing the slurred note(s) too quickly. It is best to play a new musical piece without any slurs; instead, simply pluck all of the notes with the right hand to hear the rhythm correctly, and then strive to reproduce that rhythm with the slurs.

In Example 49, the squiggly line before the notes means to *roll* the chord; that is, perform a very fast arpeggiation of the chord. Generally, aim to play the top note on the beat, with the lower notes sounding just before the beat. Notice that there are three distinct textures in this piece: measures 1–4 are chordal, measures 5–8 contain a single-note melody, and measures 9–12 contain a bass/melody texture (of course, the last measure is a chord). Pay attention to the dynamics and, for the last chord, hammer on all three fingers (do not use your right hand at all).

Example 49 - *Almost Remembered*

TRACK 36

*Played with
left hand only.

CHAPTER 10
Trills

A trill is a musical ornament, a little device that can be used to add a bit of interest to a moment of music. A trill is an alternation of a note and the next higher note in the scale. The number of times the notes alternate depends on the musical setting; in a fast piece, they may only be played once each, while, in a slow piece, the may be alternated many times, often increasing the speed (accelerando) as the trill continues. In baroque music, the trill begins on the higher note. Trills are very often simply hammer-ons and pull-offs, which, of course, are performed on a single string; however, a really impressive and effective way to perform trills is by using cross-string trills. This technique allows both notes to sound, which results in a dissonant yet pleasing (to my ears, anyway) sound. Cross-string trills cannot be played in every key, or in every instance, yet many times they are available if you look hard enough. The Bach Andante in the Repertoire for Gigs section of this book (Appendix 3) offers many opportunities for cross-string trills. Example 50 is how a typical trill would be written, followed by several different ways of playing it. Be sure to listen to the CD to hear how these examples should sound.

Example 50

Example 51 — TRACK 37

Example 52 — TRACK 38

Example 53 — TRACK 39

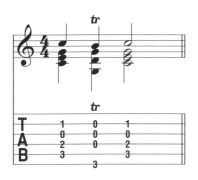

Example 54 — TRACK 40

Example 55 — TRACK 41

Example 56 — TRACK 42

Example 57 — TRACK 43

Example 58 — TRACK 44

AFTERWORD

Well, there it is: "How to play classical guitar." There are a few more techniques that we haven't discussed here, such as tremolo, rasgueado, golpe, and other easily misspelled words; however, these techniques are used only in certain types of music, notably flamenco (although, as I have stressed in this book, any technique can sound good in many styles of music). You can now take your ability on steel-string guitar bravely into the world of nylon strings.

As I said at the beginning, don't feel that now you must play only music written by Europeans 200 years ago (although much of that music is incredibly beautiful). The techniques we have learned here can be applied to any style of music that is played on a classical guitar. My suggestion is to buy several anthologies of classical-guitar music and start woodshedding. And, of course, create your own arrangements! If you know the chords and the melody of any song, you can use the techniques that you learned in this book to make it sound good in a nylon-string solo setting. Try it with songs by the Beatles, the Police, Michael Jackson, Burt Bacharach, Henry Mancini... The list is literally endless. I have even performed "Sweet Home Alabama" on a gig (on a dare) immediately after playing some Bach. A great technique is to make a song slightly more complex as it develops: start with block chords, add some arpeggios in the second verse, perhaps play the melody with rest strokes and the chords with free strokes in the chorus... Any of these tricks will make your playing more *interesting* and, consequently, your audience more *interested*. Have fun!

APPENDIX 1
Positioning the Guitar

When seated, the steel-string guitar is generally placed on the right leg. This position puts the soundhole, or pickups, slightly to our right. This position also makes the neck either point down or parallel to the ground, requiring the left arm to move from the shoulder and from the elbow to reach from the body of the guitar to the nut. When playing a classical guitar, the left foot is elevated by placing it on a footstool and placing the guitar on the left thigh with the neck angled slightly up. (In general, the headstock should be approximately at the level of your neck or head.) One result of this position is that the right hand is now at a different angle relative to the strings than it is on a steel-string guitar. Classical-guitar strings are slightly farther apart from each other than most steel-string guitars, which tend to affect one's playing style. For example, when I try to play a steel-string guitar on my left leg, it feels awkward and unnatural, but a classical guitar feels perfectly at home there. However, many players *do* place a steel-string guitar in the classical position.

There are alternative ways of getting the guitar in the correct position. I have developed back problems from using the footstool, as have many other players. When using the footstool, the guitarist's hips are out of alignment; one leg is raised, while the other isn't. One way to avoid the footstool is to use a strap. You may have seen Willie Nelson playing guitar; he uses a traditional classical-guitar strap, which is worn around the neck and has only one end, which wraps around the bottom of the guitar and hooks on the bottom (treble side) of the soundhole. This type of strap does not offer a lot of stability. I prefer to use a regular guitar strap, but certain modifications need to be made to your guitar to use this type of strap. Steel-string acoustic guitars all have an end pin at the bottom of the guitar to attach a strap to. (An acoustic guitar with a pickup generally has the output jack in place of the end pin.) There is normally a strap pin screwed into the heel of the neck, too. Many high-end acoustic guitars (Martin, Taylor, etc.) do not come from the manufacturer with this neck pin, but most players have one installed. If your classical guitar has a pickup (which I highly recommend if you want to play any gigs with it), it probably already has the end pin/output jack. If you want to use a regular guitar strap, you will need to have a good repair person install a strap pin on the neck heel. Be very careful when you have this done; some neck heels are very thin. If you do not want to screw in the strap pin on the neck heel, you can tie the strap to the headstock of the guitar, but this offers less stability.

The strap solves many stability problems and, of course, allows you to play standing up, if that is called for. But there are disadvantages: While classical guitars are very light, the weight of the right arm resting on the guitar can put quite a strain on your left shoulder, where the strap crosses your body. Other alternatives are devices that are placed between the guitar and your left thigh. I currently use such a device: a "Neck-up" attaches to the guitar with large suction cups and is adjustable for guitar angle and height. There are also vinyl "pillows" that curve to fit your thigh, "pegs" that attach with a suction cup, and several other types of devices. None of these are perfect; each has its strengths and weaknesses.

APPENDIX 2
Major Scales

Open-string forms

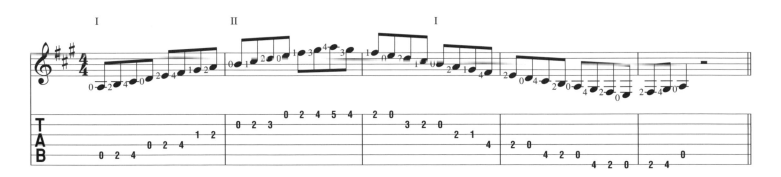

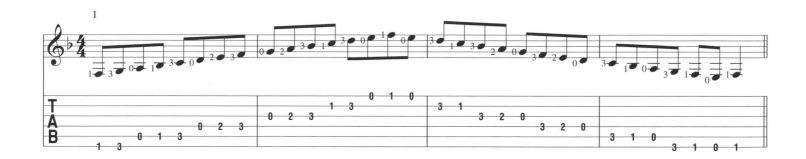

Moveable forms

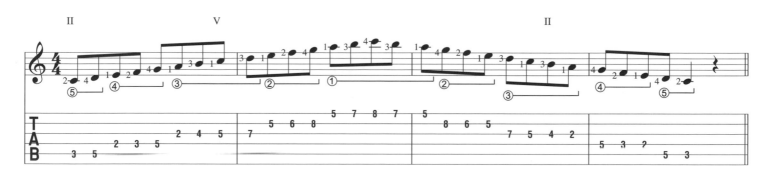

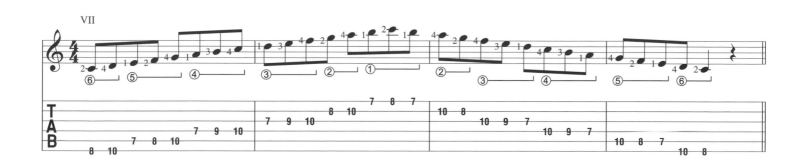

APPENDIX 3
Repertoire for Gigs

Any of the "final versions" of the examples in this book would be great for gigs, as would the original pieces at the end of each chapter. To make your life easier, here is a list of these songs:

Song	Composer	Page
A Minor Consideration	Fitzhugh	17
November	Fitzhugh	26
Prelude Op. 114	Carulli	31
Jarun	Fitzhugh	36
Study in A Minor	Aguado	41
Prelude in A Minor, Opus 114 #7	Carulli	42
Allegro Opus 48, #5	Giuliani	44
Winter Light	Fitzhugh	46
Circus	Fitzhugh	51
Variations on "La Folia"	Fitzhugh	54
Conversation	Fitzhugh	56
Almost Remembered	Fitzhugh	58

The following section is more gig material. Some was originally written for guitar; some was arranged by me from well-known themes. They all use techniques that were presented in this book and are fairly easy to play. If you can play all of the examples in the book, you can play these songs. Again, I can't stress enough: *Create your own arrangements of songs that you already know!*

"Andante" from BWV 1004

This beautiful piece is from J.S. Bach's *Second Sonata for Solo Violin*. Feel free to trill like there's no tomorrow! Baroque music sounds great with lots of trills. I have written a few trills in the tab staff, which are merely suggestions. Use any of the trill techniques that you want here.

By J.S. Bach
arr. Fitzhugh

Piano Sonata K. 331, 1st movement

In this piece, pay attention to the open fourth string; try to make it blend with the rest of the chords. On the repeats, vary the tone; play closer to the bridge *(sul ponticello)* one time, and then closer to the neck *(sul tasto)* the other time.

By W.A. Mozart
arr. Fitzhugh

Etude #3, Opus 60

This is a beautiful arpeggio piece. Notice the decrescendos as the melody moves from non-chord tones to chord tones. Feel free to either use rest stroke or a full-bodied free stroke for the melody. The entire piece is triplets; count: "one-tri-plet, two-tri-plet, three-tri-plet, four-tri-plet". The tempo marking means "slowly, but not *too* slowly." The *sf* in measure 6 means to attack that note louder; of course, the *p* indicates dynamics, not right-hand technique.

By Matteo Carcassi

Spanish Romance

Well, here it is—the "Sweet Home Alabama" of classical guitar. No matter where you play, someone will want to hear this composition. It really is a lovely piece and a great *a–m–i* arpeggio study. Here are a few things to pay attention to: bring out the melody with a strong *a* finger (preferably a free stroke so string 2 can ring). In measure 22, lift your fourth finger before placing it on the D♯, and lift it again before replacing it on the C♯. In measure 27, be sure to not place the whole chord at once with your left hand; instead, use sequential placement: fingers 4, 1, and 2, respectively. The song is generally played AABBA (play the first section once again after the repeat of the second section). And don't mistake the triplets' 3's for fingerings.

Anonymous

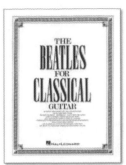

CLASSICAL GUITAR
PUBLICATIONS FROM HAL LEONARD

THE BEATLES FOR CLASSICAL GUITAR

Includes 20 solos from big Beatles hits arranged for classical guitar, complete with left-hand and right-hand fingering. Songs include: All My Loving • And I Love Her • Can't Buy Me Love • Fool on the Hill • From a Window • Hey Jude • If I Fell • Let It Be • Michelle • Norwegian Wood • Obla Di • Ticket to Ride • Yesterday • and more. Features arrangements and an introduction by Joe Washington, as well as his helpful hints on classical technique and detailed notes on how to play each song. The book also covers parts and specifications of the classical guitar, tuning, and Joe's "Strata System" – an easy-reading system applied to chord diagrams.

_____00699237 Classical Guitar $16.95

MATTEO CARCASSI – 25 MELODIC AND PROGRESSIVE STUDIES, OP. 60 • arr. Paul Henry

One of Carcassi's (1792-1853) most famous collections of classical guitar music – indispensable for the modern guitarist's musical and technical development. Performed by Paul Henry. 49-minute audio accompaniment.

_____00696506 Book/CD Pack $17.95

CLASSICAL & FINGERSTYLE GUITAR TECHNIQUES

INCLUDES TAB

by David Oakes • Musicians Institute
This Master Class with MI instructor David Oakes is aimed at any electric or acoustic guitarist who wants a quick, thorough grounding in the essentials of classical and fingerstyle technique. Topics covered include: arpeggios and scales, free stroke and rest stroke, P-i scale technique, three-to-a-string patterns, natural and artificial harmonics, tremolo and rasgueado, and more. The book includes 12 intensive lessons for right and left hand in standard notation & tab, and the CD features 92 solo acoustic tracks.

_____00695171 Book/CD Pack $14.95

CLASSICAL GUITAR CHRISTMAS COLLECTION

INCLUDES TAB

Includes classical guitar arrangements in standard notation and tablature for more than two dozen beloved carols: Angels We Have Heard on High • Auld Lang Syne • Ave Maria • Away in a Manger • Canon in D • The First Noel • God Rest Ye Merry, Gentlemen • Hark! the Herald Angels Sing • I Saw Three Ships • Jesu, Joy of Man's Desiring • Joy to the World • O Christmas Tree • O Holy Night • Silent Night • What Child Is This? • and more.

_____00699493 Guitar Solo $9.95

CLASSICAL MASTERPIECES FOR GUITAR

INCLUDES TAB

27 works by Bach, Beethoven, Handel, Mendelssohn, Mozart and more transcribed with standard notation and tablature. Now anyone can enjoy classical material regardless of their guitar background. Also features stay-open binding.

_____00699312 ....$12.95

FOR MORE INFORMATION, SEE YOUR LOCAL MUSIC DEALER,
OR WRITE TO:

HAL•LEONARD®
CORPORATION

7777 W. BLUEMOUND RD. P.O. BOX 13819 MILWAUKEE, WI 53213
Visit Hal Leonard Online at **www.halleonard.com**
Prices, contents and availability subject to change without notice.

CLASSICAL THEMES

INCLUDES TAB

20 beloved classical themes arranged for easy guitar in large-size notes (with the note names in the note heads) and tablature. Includes: Air on the G String (Bach) • Ave Maria (Schubert) • Für Elise (Beethoven) • In the Hall of the Mountain King (Grieg) • Jesu, Joy of Man's Desiring (Bach) • Largo (Handel) • Ode to Joy (Beethoven) • Pomp and Circumstance (Elgar) • and more. Ideal for beginning or vision-impaired players.

_____00699272 E-Z Play Guitar $8.95

MASTERWORKS FOR GUITAR

INCLUDES TAB

Over 60 Favorites from Four Centuries • World's Great Classical Music
Dozens of classical masterpieces: Allemande • Bourree • Canon in D • Jesu, Joy of Man's Desiring • Lagrima • Malaguena • Mazurka • Piano Sonata No. 14 in C# Minor (Moonlight) Op. 27 No. 2 First Movement Theme • Ode to Joy • Prelude No. I (Well-Tempered Clavier).

_____00699503 ....$16.95

A MODERN APPROACH TO CLASSICAL GUITAR • by Charles Duncan

This multi-volume method was developed to allow students to study the art of classical guitar within a new, more contemporary framework. For private, class or self-instruction. Book One incorporates chord frames and symbols, as well as a recording to assist in tuning and to provide accompaniments for at-home practice. Book One also introduces beginning fingerboard technique and music theory. Book Two and Three build upon the techniques learned in Book One.

_____00695114 Book 1 – Book Only...$6.95
_____00695113 Book 1 – Book/CD Pack...$10.95
_____00695116 Book 2 – Book Only...$6.95
_____00695115 Book 2 – Book/CD Pack...$10.95
_____00699202 Book 3 – Book Only...$7.95
_____00695117 Book 3 – Book/CD Pack...$10.95
_____00695119 Composite Book/CD Pack...$24.95

ANDRES SEGOVIA – 20 STUDIES FOR GUITAR • Sor/Segovia

20 studies for the classical guitar written by Beethoven's contemporary, Fernando Sor, revised, edited and fingered by the great classical guitarist Andres Segovia. These essential repertoire pieces continue to be used by teachers and students to build solid classical technique. Features a 50-minute demonstration CD.

_____00695012 Book/CD Pack $17.95
_____00006363 Book Only...$6.95

THE FRANCISCO TÁRREGA COLLECTION

INCLUDES TAB

edited and performed by Paul Henry
Considered the father of modern classical guitar, Francisco Tárrega revolutionized guitar technique and composed a wealth of music that will be a cornerstone of classical guitar repertoire for centuries to come. This unique book/CD pack features 14 of his most outstanding pieces in standard notation and tab, edited and performed on CD by virtuoso Paul Henry. Includes: Adelita • Capricho Árabe • Estudio Brillante • Grand Jota • Lágrima • Malagueña • María • Recuerdos de la Alhambra • Tango • and more, plus bios of Tárrega and Henry.

_____00698993 Book/CD Pack $17.95

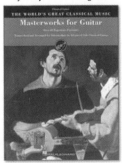